Sports Illustrated KIDS

A SUPERFAN'S GUIDE TO

PRO Football TEAMS

▶▶▶▶▶▶▶▶▶▶▶

By Drew Lyon

CAPSTONE PRESS
a capstone imprint

Sports Illustrated Kids Pro Sports Team Guides are published by Capstone Press, a Capstone Imprint, 1710 Roe Crest Drive, North Mankato, Minnesota 56003. www.capstonepub.com

Library of Congress Cataloging-in-Publication Data
is available on the Library of Congress website:
ISBN: 978-1-5157-8852-2 (library binding)
ISBN: 978-1-5157-8858-4 (eBook PDF)

Editorial Credits
Elizabeth Johnson and Nate LeBoutillier, editors; Terri Poburka, designer; Eric Gohl, media research; Gene Bentdahl, production specialist

Photo Credits
Dreamstime: Jerry Coli, 46l, 53r, 66l; Getty Images: Stringer/George Rose, 64l; Newscom: Cal Sport Media/Chris Szagola, 52r, Cal Sport Media/Craig Lassig, 44r, Cal Sport Media/Damon Tarver, 60r, Cal Sport Media/Kostas Lymperopoulos, 11l, EPA/John G. Mabanglo, 55l, EPA/Rhona Wise, 42r, EPA/Tannen Maury, 67l, Icon SMI/Todd Kirkland, 9l, Icon Sportswire/Andrew Dieb, 64r, Icon Sportswire/Andy Lewis, 68r, Icon Sportswire/John Korduner, 40r, Icon Sportswire/John Rivera, 39l, Icon Sportswire/Ken Murray, 6r, Icon Sportswire/Mark LoMoglio, 17l, Icon Sportswire/Rich Graessle, 51l, Icon Sportswire/Robin Alam, 61l, 66r, Icon Sportswire/Shelley Lipton, 43l, TNS/Max Faulkner, 56r, UPI/AJ Sisco, 26r, UPI/Bill Greenblatt, 41l, UPI/Terry Schmitt, 54r, USA Today Sports/Andrew Weber, 20r, USA Today Sports/Eric Hartline, 23l, ZUMA Press/Carlos Gonzalez, 45l, ZUMA Press/Scott A. Miller, 30r, ZUMA Press/Tampa Bay Times, 65l, ZUMA Press/Tom Rothenberg, 12r; Shutterstock: Africa Studio, throughout (helmet & football), Chones, throughout (trophies), David Lee, cover (top), Mega Pixel, throughout (pennant), Mike Flippo, 70–71bkg, 72; Sports Illustrated: Al Tielemans, 3m, 7l, 13l, 14r, 15r, 27l, 36r, 43r, 48r, 49l, 57l, 58r, Andy Hayt, 16l, 21r, 24l, 39r, 41r, 45r, 50l, 54l, 57r, 61r, Bill Frakes, 3r, 10l, 32l, 34l, 34r, 35l, 35r, 48l, Bob Rosato, 30r, 46r, 60l, 69r, Damian Strohmeyer, 8l, 22r, 27r, 47r, 65r, 67r, David E. Klutho, 16r, 32r, 33l, Heinz Kluetmeier, 14l, 18l, 42l, 70t, John Biever, 2l, 19l, 28r, 29r, 31r, 33r, 70br, John D. Hanlon, 12l, John G. Zimmerman, 6l, 51r, John Iacono, 13r, 17r, 25r, 28l, 36l, 53l, 68l, John W. McDonough, 7r, 31l, 37l, 63l, Manny Millan, 38l, 49r, 52l, 62l, Mark Kauffman, 26l, 40l, Neil Leifer, 23r, Peter Read Miller, 3l, 11r, 24r, 37r, 70bl, Richard Meek, 4–5, Robert Beck, 25l, 29l, 47l, 62r, 63r, Simon Bruty, cover (bottom), 2m, 2r, 8r, 9r, 10r, 15l, 18r, 21l, 38r, 50r, 56l, 59l, 69l, Walter Iooss Jr., 19r, 20l, 22l, 44l, 55r, 58l, 59r

Design Elements: Shutterstock

All statistics are calculated through the 2016 NFL season.

Printed in Canada
010395F17

TABLE OF CONTENTS

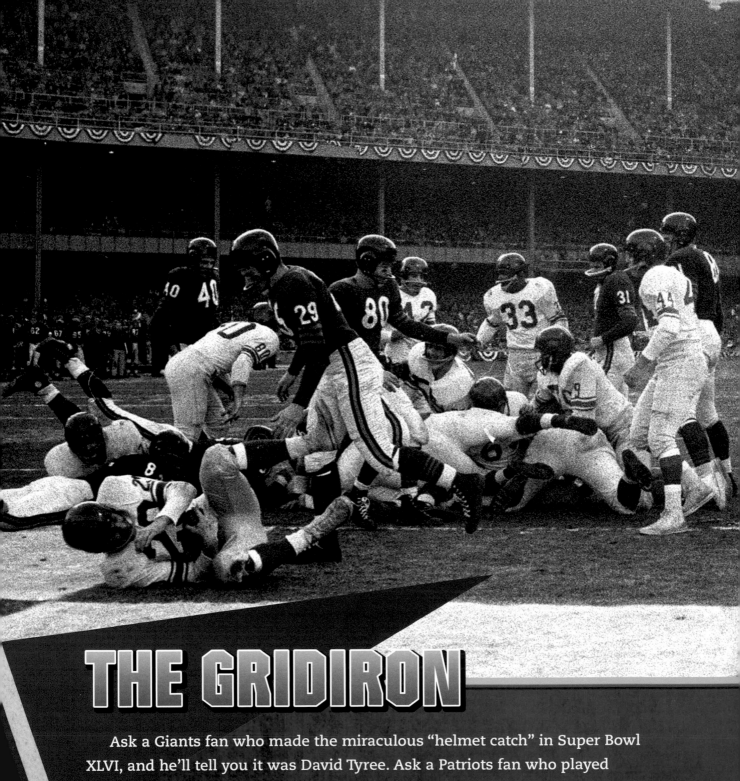

THE GRIDIRON

Ask a Giants fan who made the miraculous "helmet catch" in Super Bowl XLVI, and he'll tell you it was David Tyree. Ask a Patriots fan who played quarterback before Tom Brady, and she'll tell you it was Drew Bledsoe. Ask a Bears fan who won the only Super Bowl MVP in franchise history, and she'll tell you it was Richard Dent, the first defensive player ever to win that award.

Football fans are devoted to their favorite teams. They know all the players' names and faces, all the crucial dates and big records. They're loyal

through bad times, always feeling sure things will be different next year. That's what it means to be a fan.

It's something else to be a superfan. What's the difference? Superfans want to know it all. They steep themselves in the stories and numbers that tell the story of the National Football League (NFL). They check the results of every game and track the standings all season. They follow every team. They can't get enough.

Arizona
CARDINALS

The Arizona franchise is one of the two original National Football League franchises still operating today. The Cardinals were born in Chicago, but have called Arizona home since 1988. Riding the dynamic duo of Kurt Warner and Larry Fitzgerald, the Cardinals nearly won their first Super Bowl in 2008, but lost in the final seconds. The franchise hasn't won the league championship since 1947, currently the longest title drought in North American professional sports.

WON/LOSS RECORD:
542-732-40 (.428 W-L%)

HOME FIELD:
University of Phoenix Stadium

SUPERFACT

The Cardinals have sported roughly the same logo since 1947 — a cardinal's head on a white background. In 2006 they wore red pants for the first time in franchise history.

Then & Now

OLLIE MATSON 1952–58 / DAVID JOHNSON 2015–present

TROPHY CASE

Super Bowl Runners-Up: **XLIII**

Franchise Leaders:

Single-season receptions:
Larry Fitzgerald, 109

Single season-postseason touchdown receptions:
Larry Fitzgerald, 7 (NFL record)

Consecutive games with a touchdown pass:
Kurt Warner, 22

Longest kickoff return:
David Johnson, 108 yards

Career touchdowns:
Larry Fitzgerald, 104

SUPERFACT

Arizona receiver **Larry Fitzgerald** has been the face of the Cardinals since he was drafted in the first round in 2004. In Super Bowl XLIII "Fitz" caught two touchdown passes and was nearly the game's MVP. Fitzgerald has caught touchdown passes from 12 different Arizona quarterbacks throughout his career. When he was a kid, Fitzgerald was a ball boy for the Minnesota Vikings and was mentored by Randy Moss and future Hall of Fame receiver Cris Carter.

Atlanta
FALCONS

The Atlanta Falcons have been in the NFL since 1966. They've made two Super Bowls. Most recently, the Falcons advanced to the title game following the 2016 season. They led 28-3 in the second half before the New England Patriots came back to defeat them. But Atlanta won't quit. Current quarterback Matt Ryan is a team captain and possibly the best QB in franchise history. Ryan's top receiver, Julio Jones, is one of the best wideouts in today's game.

WON/LOSS RECORD:
341-437-6 (.438 W-L%)

HOME FIELD:
Mercedes-Benz Stadium

SUPERFACT

When the Falcons debuted in 1966, the center of their helmet was adorned by a black stripe bordered by two gold stripes and two white stripes. The colors were a tribute to the state's high profile college football teams, Georgia Tech and the University of Georgia.

Then & Now

TONY MARTIN 1998; 2001 / JULIO JONES 2011–present

SUPERFACT

A star was born in Atlanta in 2015. Running back **Devonta Freeman**, a 2014 fourth round draft pick, burst on the scene after running for 1,056 yards, scoring 14 touchdowns and getting named to the Pro Bowl. A native of Florida, Freeman wears number 24 in tribute to his late aunt, who was 24 years old when she passed away. He also has his aunt's name, Tamekia Brown, tattooed on his left arm.

TROPHY CASE

Super Bowl Runners-Up:
XXXIII, LI

Franchise Leaders:

Single-game passing yardage:
Matt Ryan, **503 yards**

Single-game receiving yardage:
Julio Jones, **300 yards**

Single-game rushing yardage:
Michael Turner, **220 yards**

Single-season receiving touchdowns:
Andre Rison, **15**

Single-season rushing yardage:
Jamal Anderson, **1,846 yards**

Career coaching wins:
Mike Smith, **66**

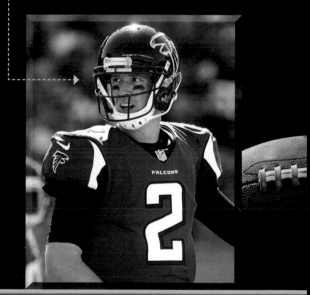

Baltimore RAVENS

Since joining the NFL in 1996, the Baltimore Ravens have often been contenders to reach the Super Bowl. Baltimore plays in the AFC North, one of football's most intense divisions. They've won the AFC championship twice, most recently in 2012. During their first Super Bowl run in 2000, they were led by an excellent defense. In 2012 they were more balanced — quarterback Joe Flacco was the MVP of the Super Bowl XLVII after he threw three touchdown passes.

WON/LOSS RECORD:
181-154-1 (.540 W-L%)

HOME FIELD:
M&T Bank Stadium

SUPERFACT

The Ravens mascot has an interesting name: Poe. The Ravens were named after a poem by Baltimore native Edgar Allan Poe. The team originally had three mascots — Edgar, Allan, and Poe. After the 2008 season, Poe became the team's sole mascot. Poe was later joined by two live ravens named Rise and Conqueror.

Then & Now

TRENT DILFER 2000 / JOE FLACCO 2008–present

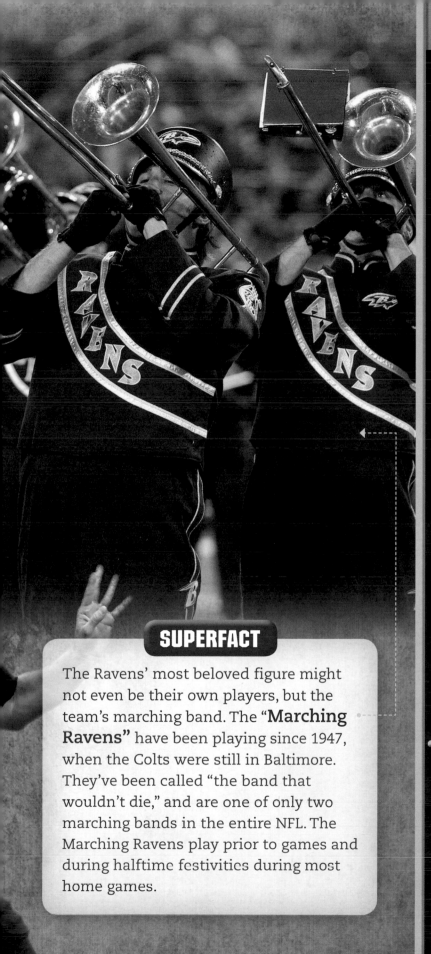

SUPERFACT

The Ravens' most beloved figure might not even be their own players, but the team's marching band. The "**Marching Ravens**" have been playing since 1947, when the Colts were still in Baltimore. They've been called "the band that wouldn't die," and are one of only two marching bands in the entire NFL. The Marching Ravens play prior to games and during halftime festivities during most home games.

TROPHY CASE

Super Bowl titles: XXXV, XLVII

Franchise Leaders:

Single-game rushing yardage:
Jamal Lewis, 295 yards

Single-season rushing yardage:
Jamal Lewis, 2,066 yards

Longest field goal:
Justin Tucker, 61 yards

Super Bowl MVPs:
Ray Lewis, Joe Flacco

Buffalo BILLS

Ignited by quarterback Jim Kelly's no-huddle offense and the steady coaching of Marv Levy, the Buffalo Bills set an NFL record during the 1990s by reaching four straight Super Bowls. The bad news? The Bills lost all four of the big games. Those Bills may not have been Super Bowl champs, but they were winners by any definition. Buffalo hasn't made the playoffs this century, but their diehard fans in upstate New York keep the faith year after year.

WON/LOSS RECORD:
400-460-8 (.465 W-L%)

HOME FIELD:
New Era Field

SUPERFACT

The Buffalo Bisons played in the All-American Football Conference in 1946. The next year, the team's owner, who owned the Frontier Oil Company, held a contest to rename the team. The team eventually settled on the Bills as a tip of the cap to Buffalo Bill Cody, a western frontiersman, even though the Bills play in upstate New York.

Then & Now
O.J. SIMPSON 1969–77 / LESEAN MCCOY 2015–present

TROPHY CASE

Super Bowl Runners-Up:
XXV, XXVI, XXVII, XXVIII

Franchise Leaders:

Largest comeback win:
32 points (NFL record)

Single-game rushing yardage:
O.J. Simpson, 273 yards

Career rushing yardage:
Thurman Thomas, 11,938 yards

Career receptions:
Andre Reed, 941

Career touchdown passes:
Jim Kelly, **237**

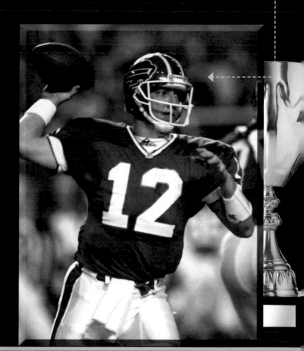

SUPERFACT

Before an injury slowed his 2016 season, Bills wideout **Sammy Watkins** was on the fast track to stardom. He racked up 15 touchdown passes and more than 2,000 receiving yards during his first two seasons. Sammy's older brother, Jaylen Watkins, plays defensive back for the Philadelphia Eagles.

Carolina
PANTHERS

The Carolina Panthers debuted in 1995 and finished 7-9, a record number of wins for an expansion team. The next season they reached the NFC title game. Carolina advanced to the Super Bowl in 2003, losing in the final seconds to the New England Patriots. With All-Pro quarterback Cam Newton guiding the team, Carolina played in Super Bowl 50, but lost again, this time to the Denver Broncos.

WON/LOSS RECORD:
172-179-1 (.490 W-L%)

HOME FIELD:
Bank of America Stadium

SUPERFACT

When the Panthers' uniforms underwent a slight alteration in 2012, they paid tribute to their former linebacker Sam Mills by placing the phrase "keep pounding" inside the jersey collar. It was Mills' motto and has since become a Carolina slogan.

Then & Now

STEVE SMITH 2001–13 / GREG OLSEN 2011–present

SUPERFACT

Cam Newton is the perhaps the key reason why the Panthers reached Super Bowl 50. The quarterback from Auburn University has speed, mobility, size, and a strong arm. He is one of the most feared quarterbacks in football. His list of achievements is growing each year. In 2015 Newton was named the NFL's MVP after he threw for 35 touchdowns and ran for 10 touchdowns.

TROPHY CASE

Super Bowl Runners-Up:
XXXVIII, 50

Franchise Leaders:

Single-game passing yardage:
Cam Newton, 432 yards

Single-game rushing yardage:
DeAngelo Williams, 210 yards

Single-season passing yardage:
Steve Beuerlein, 4,436 yards

Single-season receptions:
Steve Smith, 103

Single-season QB rating:
Jake Delhomme, 111.8 (2007)

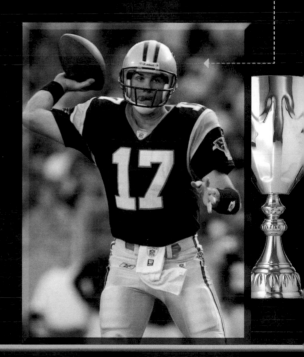

Chicago BEARS

The Chicago Bears have been members of the National Football League since 1920. They have more players in the Pro Football Hall of Fame than any other team, and also have recorded the most wins in the league history. Their only Super Bowl win came in the 1985 season when the Bears sported one of the game's most feared defenses.

WON/LOSS RECORD:
744-568-42 (.565 W-L%)

HOME FIELD:
Soldier Field

SUPERFACT

When the Bears were first formed in 1920, they weren't called the Bears. They were the Decatur Staleys. After relocating in 1921, they became the Chicago Staleys, and then they were renamed once more to the Chicago Bears in 1922. The team's mascot, Staley Da Bear, pays homage to the team's origins.

Then & Now
WALTER PAYTON 1975–87 / JORDAN HOWARD 2016–present

TROPHY CASE

Super Bowl titles: XX

Franchise Leaders:

Single-game rushing yardage:
Walter Payton, 275 yards

Single-game touchdowns:
Gale Sayers, 6 (NFL record)

Career rushing yardage:
Walter Payton, 16,726 yards

Career rushing touchdowns:
Walter Payton, 110

Career sacks:
Richard Dent, 124.5

Consecutive victories as starting QB:
Jim McMahon, 25

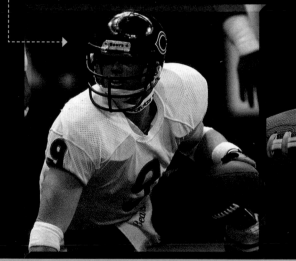

Cincinnati
BENGALS

After nearly a half-century as a franchise, the Cincinnati Bengals are still looking for their first Super Bowl title. The team hasn't even won a playoff game since 1991, even though they made the playoffs seven times in the 2000s. But the future is bright in Cincinnati with the combination of quarterback Andy Dalton and receiver A.J. Green. It's only a matter of time until the team rewards its fans with a postseason win or, better yet, a Super Bowl title.

WON/LOSS RECORD:
344-408-4 (.458 W-L%)

HOME FIELD:
Paul Brown Stadium

SUPERFACT

The Bengals' cheerleaders are called the Cincinnati Ben-Gals. In 2011 they had the league's oldest known cheerleader, Laura Vikmanis, who was 42 years old. Vikmanis was nearly 20 years older than her fellow cheerleaders.

Then & Now
DAN ROSS 1979–85 / GIOVANI BERNARD 2013–present

Wide receiver **A.J. Green** made an immediate impact on the Bengals' offense after he was drafted in 2011. Green is Andy Dalton's most trusted target, and he made the Pro Bowl in each of his first five seasons. Green could dunk a basketball by 8th grade, and he is also a juggler — he can juggle four balls at a time.

TROPHY CASE

Super Bowl Runners-Up:
XVI, XXIII

Franchise Leaders:

Single-game passing yardage:
Boomer Esiason, 490 yards

Single-season passing yardage:
Andy Dalton, 4,293 yards

Career passing touchdowns:
Ken Anderson, 197

Career rushing yardage:
Corey Dillon, 8,061 yards

Career coaching wins:
Marvin Lewis, 118

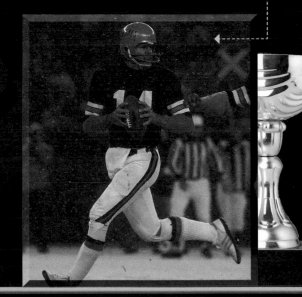

Cleveland
BROWNS

The Cleveland Browns are one of the NFL's unluckiest franchises. They have never won a Super Bowl. The Browns haven't made the playoffs since 2002, but they have a rich history dating back to the 1940s. One of the best players in NFL history, legendary running back Jim Brown, helped the Browns win their last NFL Championship in 1964. Their loyal fans can be found in the fan section at the team's home stadium, known as the "Dawg Pound."

WON/LOSS RECORD:
509-470-13 (.520 W-L%)

HOME FIELD:
FirstEnergy Stadium

SUPERFACT

The Browns were originally owned by football legend Paul Brown. Cleveland is the only NFL team named after a person, and the only team without an official helmet logo.

Then & Now
DAVE LOGAN 1976–83 / JOE HADEN 2010–present

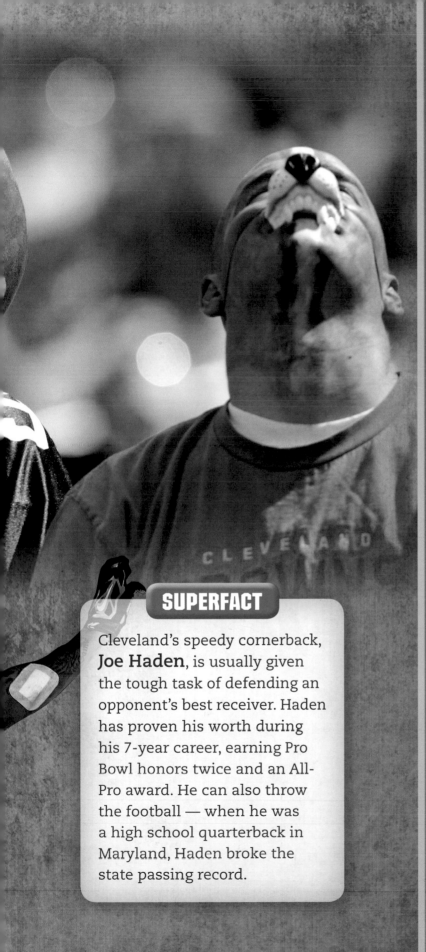

Cleveland's speedy cornerback, **Joe Haden**, is usually given the tough task of defending an opponent's best receiver. Haden has proven his worth during his 7-year career, earning Pro Bowl honors twice and an All-Pro award. He can also throw the football — when he was a high school quarterback in Maryland, Haden broke the state passing record.

TROPHY CASE

Super Bowl Appearances:
None

Franchise Leaders:

Single-game touchdowns:
Dub Jones, 6 (NFL record)

Single-season rushing yardage:
Jim Brown, 1,863 yards

Career receptions:
Ozzie Newsome, 662

Career rushing yardage:
Jim Brown, 12,312 yards

Consecutive unintercepted passes:
Bernie Kosar, 308

Dallas
COWBOYS

The Cowboys are called "America's Team" by their legion of fans across the country. They have won five Super Bowls and are considered one of the NFL's most visible franchises. The Cowboys have won just two playoff games since 1996, but they will continue to pack the stands at their new stadium, which features a video screen that is 160 feet wide!

WON/LOSS RECORD:
493-367-6 (.573 W-L%)

HOME FIELD:
AT&T Stadium

SUPERFACT

The Cowboys' blue-and-white star logo is one of the most famous in sports and has remained virtually unchanged since 1964. The star is in reference to Texas' "Lone Star State" nickname and the single star on the state flag.

Then & Now

TONY DORSETT 1977–87 / DEZ BRYANT 2010–present

TROPHY CASE

Super Bowl Titles:
VI, XII, XXVII, XXVIII, XXX

Franchise Leaders:

Single-game passing yardage:
Tony Romo, 506 yards

Career rushing yardage:
Emmitt Smith, 17,162 yards

Career touchdown passes:
Tony Romo, 248

Career touchdowns:
Emmitt Smith, 164

Most NFL touchdown passes, 1973:
Roger Staubach, 23

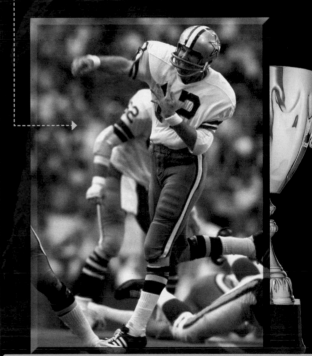

SUPERFACT

When **Dak Prescott** was drafted in the fourth round of the 2016 draft, the Cowboys were hoping he might grow into their quarterback of the future. After starting quarterback Tony Romo was injured in the 2016 preseason, Prescott quickly became the quarterback of the present. Prescott, who grew up a Cowboys fan, didn't play like a rookie. He led the Cowboys to an 11-game winning streak and a division title.

Denver
BRONCOS

The Denver Broncos are one of the NFL's most successful franchises when it comes to championships. They've appeared in eight Super Bowls and have won three, most recently winning Super Bowl 50 after the 2015 season. Their Hall of Fame quarterback, John Elway, moved to the front office after retiring and is now the team's general manager. Quarterback Peyton Manning retired after Super Bowl 50, but the Broncos' stellar defense should keep them competitive for years to come.

WON/LOSS RECORD:
465-393-10 (.535 W-L%)

HOME FIELD:
Sports Authority Field at Mile High

SUPERFACT

After every Denver home touchdown, the team's mascot tramples from end zone to end zone. It's not a human doing the running, but a purebred Arabian horse named Thunder. The original Thunder ran the field for 11 seasons before retiring at the beginning of the 2004 season.

Then & Now
STEVE WATSON 1979–87 / DEMARYIUS THOMAS 2010–present

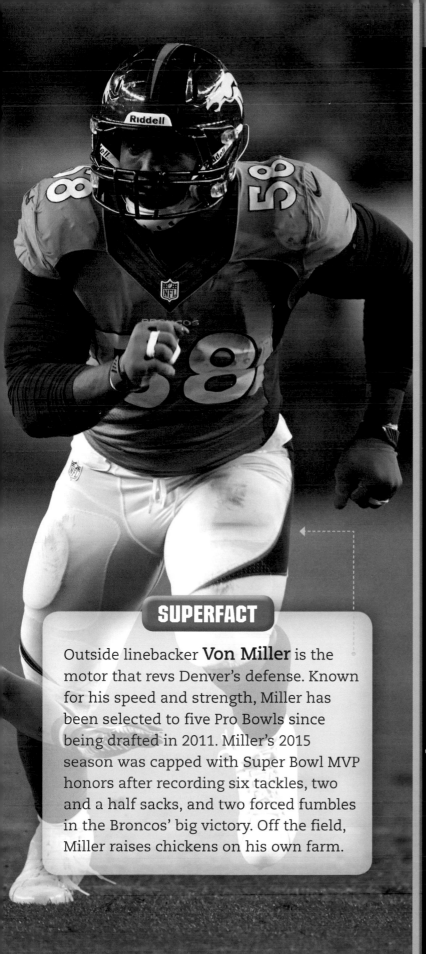

SUPERFACT

Outside linebacker **Von Miller** is the motor that revs Denver's defense. Known for his speed and strength, Miller has been selected to five Pro Bowls since being drafted in 2011. Miller's 2015 season was capped with Super Bowl MVP honors after recording six tackles, two and a half sacks, and two forced fumbles in the Broncos' big victory. Off the field, Miller raises chickens on his own farm.

TROPHY CASE

Super Bowl titles:
XXXII, XXXIII, 50

Franchise Leaders:

Single-season passing touchdowns:
Peyton Manning, 55 (NFL record)

Single-season receptions:
Rod Smith, 113

Single-season rushing yardage:
Terrell Davis, 2,008 yards

Career passing yardage:
John Elway, 51,475 yards

Longest field goal:
Matt Prater, 64 yards (NFL record)

Detroit LIONS

The Detroit Lions haven't given their long-suffering fans much to cheer about in recent decades. The Lions have never made the Super Bowl and haven't won a league championship since 1957. But after finishing 0-16 in 2008, the team drafted quarterback Matthew Stafford and has been on the upswing ever since. The Lions are no longer an NFL joke. The roar has been restored!

WON/LOSS RECORD:
544-641-32 (.460 W-L%)

HOME FIELD:
Ford Field

SUPERFACT

The Lions were originally based in Ohio and called the Portsmouth Spartans. Portsmouth was one of the smallest cities in the NFL. After four seasons the franchise moved to Michigan in 1934.

Then & Now
DOAK WALKER 1950–55 / GOLDEN TATE 2014–present

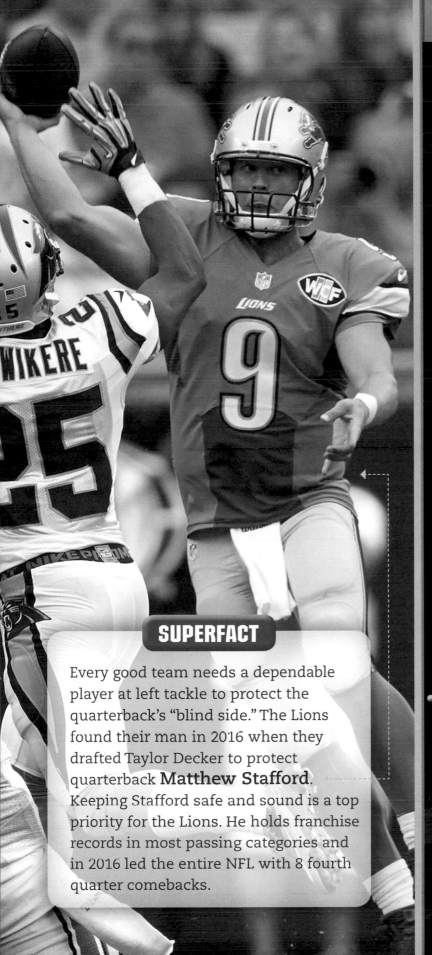

SUPERFACT

Every good team needs a dependable player at left tackle to protect the quarterback's "blind side." The Lions found their man in 2016 when they drafted Taylor Decker to protect quarterback **Matthew Stafford**. Keeping Stafford safe and sound is a top priority for the Lions. He holds franchise records in most passing categories and in 2016 led the entire NFL with 8 fourth quarter comebacks.

TROPHY CASE

Super Bowl Appearances:
None

Franchise Leaders:

Single-game receiving yardage:
Calvin Johnson, **329 yards**

Single-game rushing yardage:
Barry Sanders, 237 yards

Single-season passing touchdowns:
Matthew Stafford, 41

Single-season receiving yardage:
Calvin Johnson, 1,964 yards

Single-season rushing yardage:
Barry Sanders, 2,053 yards

Green Bay
PACKERS

The Packers reside in "Titletown U.S.A.," also known as Green Bay, Wisconsin. They have one of the league's most loyal fanbases and 13 league championships — most recently Super Bowl XLV. Packers fans, also known as "Cheeseheads," have had plenty to cheer about since quarterback Aaron Rodgers replaced Hall of Famer Brett Favre in 2008. With the All-Pro Rodgers under center, the Packers always have a chance.

WON/LOSS RECORD:
730-553-37 (.567 W-L%)

HOME FIELD:
Lambeau Field

SUPERFACT

Though stock is not currently available for purchase, many Packer fans are part owners of their favorite team. The franchise has roughly 360,000 shareholders. It is the only nonprofit pro sports franchise in the U.S. Each year, the team holds a shareholders meeting at Lambeau Field.

Then & Now

DESMOND HOWARD 1996; 1999 / JORDY NELSON 2008–present

SUPERFACT

The Packers drafted **Aaron Rodgers** in 2005 to succeed their star quarterback, Brett Favre. Rodgers waited his turn and was handed the keys to the Packers in 2008. It became clear that Rodgers was a star—his arm may be the strongest in NFL history. Rodgers was the MVP of Super Bowl XLV and will be the key to bringing another championship to Titletown. When he's not shredding defenses, Rodgers is an avid video game player.

TROPHY CASE

Super Bowl titles: I, II, XXXI, XLV

NFL MVPs:
Paul Hornung, Jim Taylor, Bart Starr, Brett Favre, Aaron Rodgers

Franchise Leaders:

Single-season touchdown passes:
Aaron Rodgers, 45

Single-season touchdown receptions:
Sterling Sharpe, 18

Consecutive games:
Brett Favre, **255**

Career touchdown passes:
Brett Favre, 442

Career wins:
Brett Favre, 160

Houston
TEXANS

The Houston Texans are the NFL's youngest franchise. They played their first game in 2002 and won their first playoff game in 2011. They've won the AFC South four times. The Texans hoped they found their leader of the future in 2017, when they drafted Clemson quarterback Deshaun Watson in the NFL Draft.

WON/LOSS RECORD:
106-134 (.442 W-L%)

HOME FIELD:
NRG Stadium

SUPERFACT

Before deciding to name the team the Texans, Houston had four other team names to consider: the Apollos, Bobcats, Stallions and Wildcatters. Dallas once had an American Football League team called the Texans, and Houston owner Bob McNair had to get permission to use the name.

Then & Now

ANDRE JOHNSON 2003–14 / JADEVEON CLOWNEY 2014–present

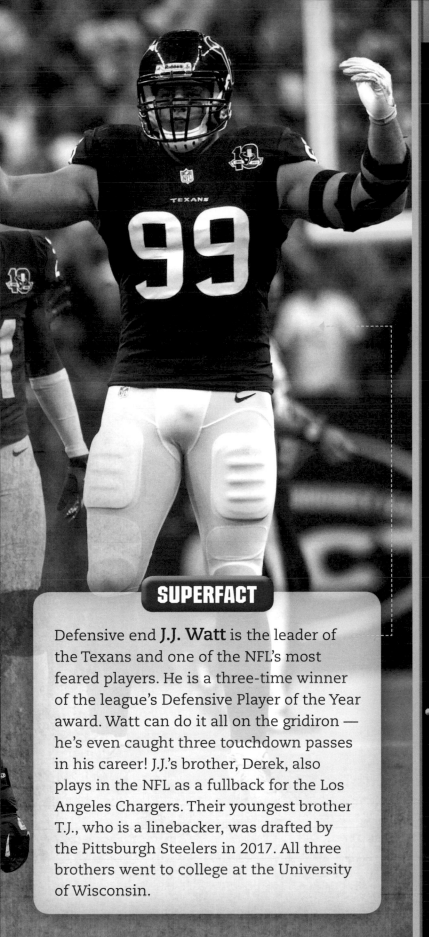

SUPERFACT

Defensive end **J.J. Watt** is the leader of the Texans and one of the NFL's most feared players. He is a three-time winner of the league's Defensive Player of the Year award. Watt can do it all on the gridiron — he's even caught three touchdown passes in his career! J.J.'s brother, Derek, also plays in the NFL as a fullback for the Los Angeles Chargers. Their youngest brother T.J., who is a linebacker, was drafted by the Pittsburgh Steelers in 2017. All three brothers went to college at the University of Wisconsin.

TROPHY CASE

Super Bowl Appearances:
None

Franchise Leaders:

Single-season receptions:
Andre Johnson, 115

Single-season rushing touchdowns:
Arian Foster, 16

Single-season quarterback sacks:
J.J. Watt, 20.5

Career receptions:
Andre Johnson, 1,012

Inaugural starting quarterback:
David Carr, 2002

Indianapolis
COLTS

The Colts have been in the league since 1953, and moved from Baltimore to Indianapolis after the 1983 season. They have appeared in the playoffs 27 times. Two of the NFL's best quarterbacks, Peyton Manning and Johnny Unitas, have worn the team's horseshoe logo. The Colts last won the NFC South Division in 2014.

WON/LOSS RECORD:
502-441-7 (.532 W-L%)

HOME FIELD:
Lucas Oil Stadium

SUPERFACT

Legendary quarterback Johnny Unitas was famous for wearing black high top shoes, which were unusual for his time. After Unitas died in 2002, Peyton Manning wanted to honor him by wearing black high tops, but the NFL told Manning he would be violating the league's strict uniform codes and would face a $25,000 fine.

Then & Now
MARVIN HARRISON 1996–2008 / T.Y. HILTON 2012–present

TROPHY CASE

Super Bowl titles: V, XLI

Franchise Leaders:

Single-season receptions:
**Marvin Harrison, 143
(NFL record)**

Career touchdown passes:
Peyton Manning, 399

Career receptions:
Marvin Harrison, 1,102

Career rushing yardage:
Edgerrin James, 9,226 yards

First Colt elected to the Hall of Fame:
Art Donovan, 1968

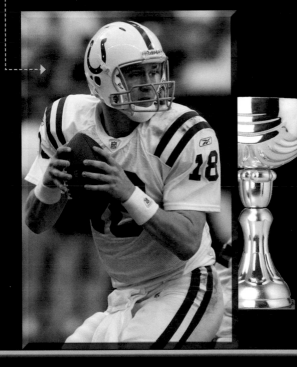

SUPERFACT

Andrew Luck was faced with some big shoes to fill when he was drafted first overall in the 2012 draft to replace the legendary Peyton Manning. Luck proved worthy of the top selection — he has made the Pro Bowl three times and was the NFL's passing touchdown leader in 2014. Off the field, Luck loves reading and often recommends books to his teammates.

Jacksonville
JAGUARS

Founded in 1995, the Jacksonville Jaguars took a bite out of the league by reaching the AFC Championship in just their second season. The Jags made the playoffs the following three seasons and also found success in the mid-2000s after hiring head coach Jack Del Rio. The Jaguars haven't made the playoffs since 2007 and need a spark to become contenders again.

WON/LOSS RECORD:
155-197 (.440 W-L%)

HOME FIELD:
EverBank Field

SUPERFACT

Jaxson De Ville is the Jaguars' mascot. He's known for being more flamboyant and edgy than most mascots, which has caused other teams to complain about his antics. Jaxson De Ville will sometimes parachute into the stadium.

Then & Now
MARK BRUNELL 1995-2003 / BLAKE BORTLES 2014-present

SUPERFACT

Jaguars wide receiver **Allen Robinson** made a giant step forward in his second NFL season. In 2015 he set a team record by catching 14 touchdowns and was named to the Pro Bowl. He is the favorite target of quarterback Blake Bortles. After his career Robinson hopes to become a sports commentator.

TROPHY CASE

Super Bowl Appearances:
None

Franchise Leaders:

Single-game touchdowns:
James Stewart, 5

Single-season receptions:
Jimmy Smith, 116

Career rushing yardage:
Fred Taylor, 11,271 yards

Single-season touchdown passes:
Blake Bortles, 35

Career coaching wins:
Jack Del Rio, 68

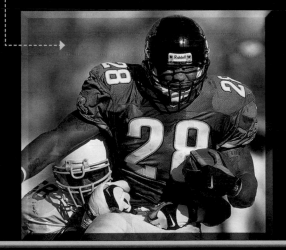

Kansas City CHIEFS

The Chiefs play in Arrowhead Stadium, one of the NFL's loudest stadiums. They played in the very first Super Bowl, coming in second to the Green Bay Packers. They won Super Bowl IV against the Minnesota Vikings, but Kansas City hasn't appeared in the big game since. Fortunately, they have made the playoffs three times since hiring head coach Andy Reid and signing quarterback Alex Smith.

WON/LOSS RECORD:
447-409-12 (.522 W-L%)

HOME FIELD:
Arrowhead Stadium

SUPERFACT

We can thank the Chiefs' original owner, Lamar Hunt, for naming the Super Bowl. Hunt recalled that he saw his daughter playing with a Super Ball, and first used the term at a league meeting in 1966 when the National Football League and American Football League were planning their first championship game.

Then & Now

PRIEST HOLMES 2001–07 / SPENCER WARE 2015–present

SUPERFACT

Alex Smith was dismissed as a bust during his first few years with the San Francisco 49ers. The former number one overall pick in the 2005 NFL Draft found a new life when he was traded to Kansas City. In 2013 he led the Chiefs to the playoffs and was selected to his first Pro Bowl. The critics don't label Smith as a bust anymore; they call him a darn good quarterback.

TROPHY CASE

Super Bowl titles: IV

Franchise Leaders:

Single-game quarterback sacks:
Derrick Thomas, 7 (NFL record)

Single-season rushing touchdowns:
Priest Holmes, 27

Career kick or punt returns for a touchdown:
Dante Hall, 11

Career passing yardage:
Len Dawson, 28,507 yards

Career receptions:
Tony Gonzalez, 916

Los Angeles
CHARGERS

The Chargers were original members of the American Football League (AFL). They joined the NFL in 1971, and featured several Hall of Famers, including receiver Lance Alworth, quarterback Dan Fouts, and linebacker Junior Seau. Quarterback Philip Rivers has been a team leader since he was drafted in 2004, bringing the Chargers to the playoffs five times in his career. The Chargers are one of 13 teams that have never won a Super Bowl.

WON/LOSS RECORD:
426-431-11 (.497 W-L%)

HOME FIELD:
StubHub Center

SUPERFACT

After 56 seasons in San Diego, the Chargers announced they were moving 120 miles north to Los Angeles after the 2016 season. The team unveiled a new "LA" logo that was similar in color and design to baseball's L.A. Dodgers' but scrapped it after just 48 hours when fans disapproved.

Then & Now
CHUCK MUNCIE 1980—84 / ANTONIO GATES 2003—present

TROPHY CASE

Super Bowl Runners-Up: XXIX

Franchise Leaders:

Single-season points:
**LaDainian Tomlinson, 186
(NFL record)**

Single-season touchdowns:
**LaDainian Tomlinson, 31
(NFL record)**

Single-season passing yardage:
Dan Fouts, 4,802

Career touchdown passes:
Philip Rivers, 314

NFL receptions in a season leader:
Kellen Winslow, 1980 & 1981

SUPERFACT

The Chargers have a history of quality tight ends. They drafted **Hunter Henry** in 2016, believing the Arkansas native was the next generation tight end for the team. Henry finished with a stellar rookie season, recording 8 touchdowns. He's tall, strong, and quick. It's a combination of the perfect ingredients for tight ends that catch a lot of passes and block big defensive players, too.

Los Angeles RAMS

The Rams returned home to Los Angeles before the 2016 season after playing 21 years in St. Louis. In 1999 they featured "The Greatest Show on Turf," a high-powered offense led by quarterback Kurt Warner that climaxed with a Super Bowl title. The Rams are looking to start fresh in the California sunshine. Running back Todd Gurley and quarterback Jared Goff may hold the keys to the team's success in Hollywood.

WON/LOSS RECORD:
544-554-21 (.496 W-L%)

HOME FIELD:
Los Angeles Memorial Coliseum

SUPERFACT

Rampage, the Rams' mascot, wears uniform number 1 and has been cheering on the team since 2010. Before Rampage came on the scene, the Rams had another mascot named Ramster. He looked more like a rat than a ram and wasn't very popular with the team's fanbase.

Then & Now

NORM VAN BROCKLIN 1949–57 / JARED GOFF 2016–present

TROPHY CASE

Super Bowl titles: XXXIV

Franchise Leaders:

Single-season rushing yardage:
Eric Dickerson, 2,105 yards
(NFL record)

Single-season passing touchdowns:
Kurt Warner, 41

Single-season touchdowns:
Marshall Faulk, 26

Single-season sacks:
Deacon Jones, 22

Career seasons:
Jackie Slater, 20

SUPERFACT

Todd Gurley had a sensational career at the University of Georgia before a knee injury sidetracked him. Still, the Rams drafted him 10th overall in 2015. Gurley lived up to the hype during his rookie year by rushing for 1,106 yards and 10 TDs and earning a Pro Bowl nod.

Miami
DOLPHINS

In the nearly 100 years of the NFL, no other team has completed the job Miami finished in 1972. From start to finish, the Dolphins won every single game. It's a record that still holds to this day. The Dolphins of today have struggled making the playoffs, but returned to the postseason in 2016. Current head coach Adam Gase might have the right formula to bring the Dolphins back to excellence. Just don't expect another perfect season.

WON/LOSS RECORD:
439-341-4 (.563 W-L%)

HOME FIELD:
Hard Rock Stadium

SUPERFACT

Lee Ofman wrote the Dolphins' original fight song in 1972. It served as a good luck charm during Miami's undefeated season of 1972 and held strong for decades. In 2009 the team debuted a new fight song, "Fins," composed by singer Jimmy Buffett. Recently, rappers T-Pain and Pitbull have made alterations to the team song.

Then & Now

BOB GRIESE 1967–80 / RYAN TANNEHILL 2012–present

TROPHY CASE

Super Bowl titles: VII, VIII

Franchise Leaders:

Single-season passing yardage:
Dan Marino, 5,084 yards

Career touchdown passes:
Dan Marino, 420

Career coaching wins:
Don Shula, 257

Longest pass:
Bob Griese, 86 yards

Career receptions:
Mark Clayton, 550

Career receiving yardage:
Mark Duper, 8,869 yards

SUPERFACT

Jay Ajayi lived in England until he moved to American when he was seven years old. He was a very skilled soccer player, but decided he liked American football even better. It was a good decision—the tailback was drafted by the Dolphins in 2015, and ran for more than 1,000 yards in his second year. The Dolphins may have found their running back of the future.

Minnesota
VIKINGS

Perhaps no team in NFL history has been more snake-bitten than the Vikings. Their story is filled with heartbreaking defeats in the biggest moments—NFC Championship games and Super Bowls. They've featured no shortage of star power throughout their history, but the Vikes are still desperately searching for their first Super Bowl trophy. After moving to new U.S. Bank Stadium in 2016, the Vikings hope their luck will turn with a change in scenery.

WON/LOSS RECORD:
457-387-10 (.541 W-L%)

HOME FIELD:
U.S. Bank Stadium

SUPERFACT

When the Vikings score during home games, the crowd breaks out into the team's official song, "Skol, Vikings." Skol is a Norwegian and Swedish term for "cheers." The jingle was written by a local composer, James "Red" McLeod, and has been chanted by Vikings fans for more than 50 years. Skol!

Then & Now

FRAN TARKENTON 1961–66; 1972–78 / ADAM THIELEN 2014–present

TROPHY CASE

Super Bowl appearances:
IV, VIII, IX, XI

Franchise Leaders:

Single-game rushing yardage:
Adrian Peterson, 296 yards (NFL record)

Career quarterback sacks:
Carl Eller, 130

Career touchdown receptions:
Cris Carter, 110

Career coaching wins:
Bud Grant, 158

Most yards receiving, playoff game:
Anthony Carter, 227 (1988)

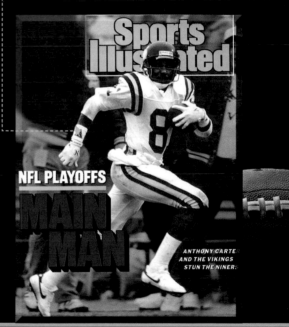

SUPERFACT

Early in his career, free safety **Harrison Smith** worked his way into position as one of the NFL's more reliable players in the defensive secondary. Smith is quick, hits hard, and has soft hands. He made his first Pro Bowl in 2015 before the Vikings signed him to a five-year contract extension. Smith is also a versatile athlete — the Tennessee native played high school basketball and ran track.

New England
PATRIOTS

The Patriots championship dynasty is unlike anything the NFL has ever seen before. Since 2001 they've played in six Super Bowls, won four, and have missed the playoffs only twice in that span. The duo of head coach Bill Belichick and quarterback Tom Brady is the most successful combination in the league's history. Brady has anchored all four Super Bowl championships, and will retire as perhaps the greatest quarterback to strap on a helmet.

WON/LOSS RECORD:
476-383-9 (.554 W-L%)

HOME FIELD:
Gillette Stadium

SUPERFACT

Pat Patriot is New England's mascot and dresses in the uniform of an American Revolutionary War soldier. Pat Patriot was the team's original logo, which was used until 1993 and designed by a newspaper cartoonist. Pat Patriot has been on the field for each of New England's four Super Bowl wins.

Then & Now

STEVE GROGAN 1975–90 / TOM BRADY 2000–present

TROPHY CASE

XXXVI, XXXVIII, XXXIX, XLIX, LI

Single-season touchdown receptions:
Randy Moss, 23 (NFL record)

Career 300-yard passing games:
Tom Brady, 72

Career regular-season wins:
Tom Brady, 183

Career coaching wins:
Bill Belichick, 201

2014 Comeback Player of the Year:
Rob Gronkowski

SUPERFACT

Julian Edelman, the Patriots' 5-foot-10 receiver has become the good buddy and favorite target of quarterback Tom Brady. Edelman is a quick and shifty pass catcher and punt returner who finds holes in tight spaces. He was a key ingredient in the Patriots' most recent Super Bowl victory.

New Orleans
SAINTS

Who Dat Nation finally saw their Saints win a Super Bowl in 2009. A high-octane offense driven by quarterback Drew Brees helped the Saints upset the Colts, sending New Orleans into party mode. After Sean Payton took over as coach in 2006 and signed Brees, the Saints became a potent offensive franchise. Before 2006 the Saints only won a single playoff game in their entire history. The Payton and Brees combination has won six playoff games.

WON/LOSS RECORD:
338-427-5 (.442 W-L%)

HOME FIELD:
Mercedes-Benz Superdome

SUPERFACT

During the 2005 season, the wreckage of Hurricane Katrina forced the Saints to play their home games at nearby Louisiana State University and also in Texas and New Jersey. They returned to their remodeled home stadium, the Superdome, for the next season, where they won their first home game after the devastating hurricane.

Then & Now

DEUCE MCALLISTER 2001–08 / MARK INGRAM 2011–present

TROPHY CASE

Super Bowl titles: XLIV

Franchise Leaders:

Single-season completions:
Drew Brees, 471 (NFL record)

Consecutive 4,000-yard seasons:
Drew Brees, 11

Consecutive games with a touchdown pass:
Drew Brees, 54 (NFL record)

Most completions in the league:
Archie Manning, 230 (1972)

New York GIANTS

The Giants have been in the NFL since 1925. They reside in the NFC's East division, and are one of the league's model franchises. They've won four Super Bowls. The Giants narrowly beat the undefeated New England Patriots in Super Bowl XLII, one of the most thrilling games in NFL history. The Giants beat the Patriots again in Super Bowl XLVI with quarterback Eli Manning leading another fourth-quarter comeback.

WON/LOSS RECORD:
684-572-33 (.543 W-L%)

HOME FIELD:
MetLife Stadium

SUPERFACT

The Giants have only used three logos in their entire history. During the 2016 season the team wore white pants and white cleats for every game for the first time since the late 1990s.

Then & Now
PHIL SIMMS 1979–93 / ELI MANNING 2004–present

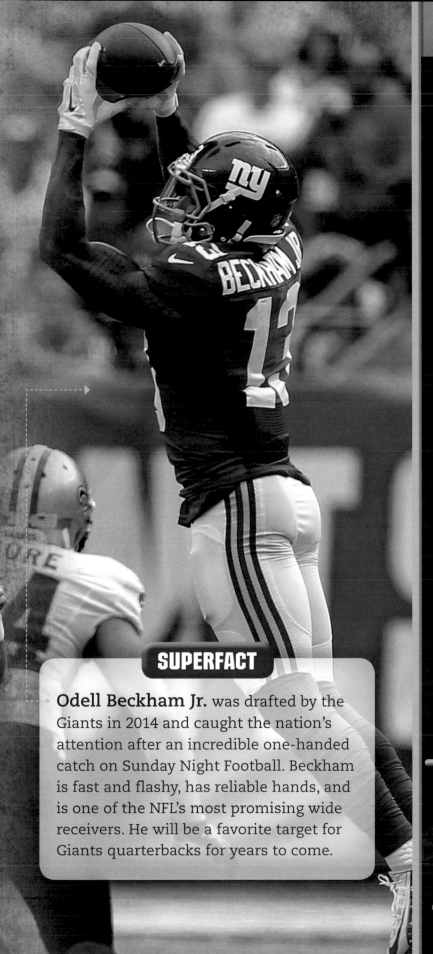

Odell Beckham Jr. was drafted by the Giants in 2014 and caught the nation's attention after an incredible one-handed catch on Sunday Night Football. Beckham is fast and flashy, has reliable hands, and is one of the NFL's most promising wide receivers. He will be a favorite target for Giants quarterbacks for years to come.

TROPHY CASE

Super Bowl titles:
XXI, XXV, XLII, XLVI

Franchise Leaders:

Single-season quarterback sacks:
Michael Strahan, 22.5 sacks (NFL record)

Career quarterback sacks:
Michael Strahan 141.5

Career rushing yardage:
Tiki Barber, 10,449 yards

Super Bowl MVPs:
Eli Manning, 2 (XLII and XLVI)

League leader, yards from scrimmage, 1956:
Frank Gifford, 1,422 yards

New York
JETS

Few football observers gave the New York Jets a fighting chance against the Baltimore Colts in Super Bowl III. Jets quarterback Joe Namath disagreed and personally guaranteed a Jets win. The Jets upset the Colts, and Namath was proven right in the most famous guarantee in sports history. The Jets reached the AFC title games in 2009 and 2010 but are still looking for their second Super Bowl win.

WON/LOSS RECORD:
392-468-8 (.456 W-L%)

HOME FIELD:
MetLife Stadium

SUPERFACT

Sonny Werblin bought the New York Titans, a struggling football franchise, in 1963. The team was renamed the Jets because the new stadium was located between JFK and La Guardia airports. The new name also rhymed with the new local baseball team, the Mets, who would share Shea Stadium with the Jets.

Then & Now
KEN O'BRIEN 1984–92 / BRYCE PETTY 2016–present

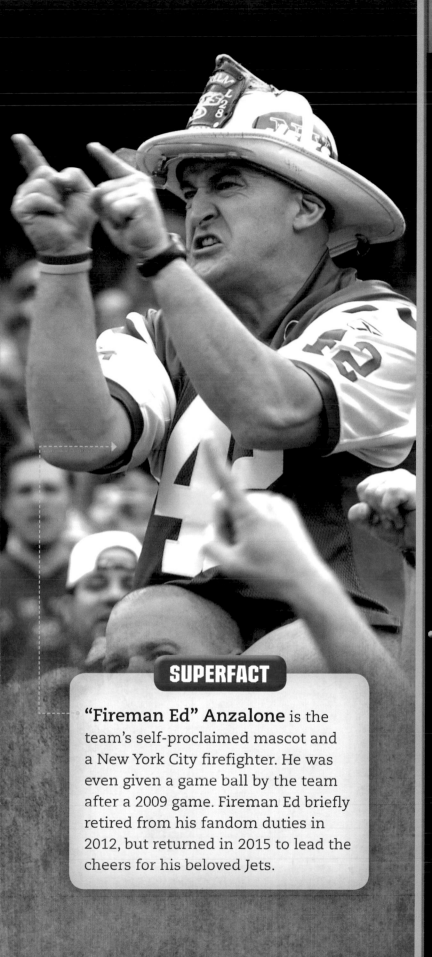

Super Bowl titles: III

Franchise Leaders:

Single-season receptions:
Brandon Marshall, 109

Single-season rushing yardage:
Curtis Martin, 1,697 yards

Career passing yardage:
Joe Namath, 27,057 yards

Career coaching wins:
Weeb Ewbank, 71

SUPERFACT

"Fireman Ed" Anzalone is the team's self-proclaimed mascot and a New York City firefighter. He was even given a game ball by the team after a 2009 game. Fireman Ed briefly retired from his fandom duties in 2012, but returned in 2015 to lead the cheers for his beloved Jets.

Oakland RAIDERS

The silver-and-black Raiders have a motto made famous by their late owner, Al Davis: "Just win, baby." During the 1970s and '80s, the Raiders' commitment to excellence led to a lot of winning, including three Super Bowls. They lost the Super Bowl following the 2002 season, however, and didn't make the playoffs again until 2016. Led by head coach Jack Del Rio and quarterback Derek Carr, the Raiders are back to winning again, baby.

WON/LOSS RECORD:
456-401-11 (.532 W-L%)

HOME FIELD:
Oakland Alameda Coliseum

SUPERFACT

The Raiders' logo and uniforms mean business. Their silver and black outfits have remained virtually unchanged since 1963 and have become a fixture in popular culture. The team's colors led the team to coin the phrase, "real men wear black."

Then & Now
MARCUS ALLEN 1982–92 / JALEN RICHARD 2016–present

SUPERFACT

The Raiders finally found their quarterback of the future when they drafted **Derek Carr** in 2014. After throwing for 32 touchdowns and earning Pro Bowl honors in 2015, Carr led the Raiders to the playoffs in 2016. Carr has a strong arm, is mobile, and is a leader in the huddle. Even though he grew up a Cowboys fan, Carr now bleeds Raider silver and black.

TROPHY CASE

Super Bowl titles:
XI, XV, XVIII

Franchise Leaders:

Single-game rushing yardage:
Napoleon Kaufman, 227

Career passing touchdowns:
Ken Stabler, 150

Career receiving touchdowns:
Tim Brown, 99

Career coaching wins:
John Madden, 103

Longest touchdown run:
Terrelle Pryor, 93 yards

Philadelphia EAGLES

People in Philadelphia love their cheesesteaks, and they really, really love their Eagles. The team has sold out every home game since 1999, but Eagles fans have yet to see their squad win a Super Bowl. They've made the playoffs 24 times, and 20 of their players have reached the Hall of Fame. Eagles fans have cause to pack the home stadium again after drafting quarterback Carson Wentz in 2016.

WON/LOSS RECORD:
555-591-26 (.485 W-L%)

HOME FIELD:
Lincoln Financial Field

SUPERFACT

Swoop is the Eagles' mascot. Swoop is a bald eagle and appears as an animated character in the team's weekly children's television show. Swoop also appeared in the film comedy *Ace Ventura: Pet Detective*.

Then & Now
DONOVAN MCNABB 1999–2009 / CARSON WENTZ 2016–present

TROPHY CASE

Super Bowl Runners-Up:
XV, XXXIX

Franchise Leaders:

Career touchdown passes:
Donovan McNabb, 216

Single-season receptions:
Brian Westbrook, 90

Single-season touchdowns:
LeSean McCoy, 20

Career quarterback sacks:
Reggie White, 124

Pittsburgh STEELERS

No team has hoisted the Super Bowl Vince Lombardi Trophy more than the Pittsburgh Steelers. They've won six Super Bowls, and are a model franchise. Since drafting Ben Roethlisberger in 2004, Pittsburgh has never been very far from the top of the AFC pack. They've won two Super Bowls during Roethlisberger's career and have reached the playoffs nine times.

WON/LOSS RECORD:
606-549-21 (.524 W-L%)

HOME FIELD:
Heinz Field

SUPERFACT

The Steelers logo, which is a tribute to the American Iron and Steel Institute, is unique in the NFL. Pittsburgh is the only team with its logo on only one side of the helmet. This move was supposed to be temporary, but the team decided to keep the logo on only one side, and leave the other side all black.

Then & Now

FRANCO HARRIS 1972–83 / LE'VEON BELL 2013–present

TROPHY CASE

Super Bowl titles:
IX, X, XIII, XIV, XL, XLIII

Franchise Leaders:

Career passing yardage:
Ben Roethlisberger, 46,814 yards

Career rushing yardage:
Franco Harris, 11,950 yards

Career receiving yardage:
Hines Ward, 12,083 yards

Career coaching wins:
Chuck Noll, 193

SUPERFACT

Antonio Brown is one of the league's most explosive receivers and Ben Roethlisberger's favorite target. Brown led the NFL in receptions for three straight seasons, and is a five-time Pro Bowl honoree. Not bad for a player who was overlooked in college and fell to the sixth round of the NFL Draft. Brown is also a smooth dancer — he shows off his moves after touchdowns. He also competed in the television series "Dancing with the Stars."

San Francisco
49ERS

The 49ers were the team of the 1980s. If they didn't win the Super Bowl in that decade, the season was considered a failure. With Hall of Fame quarterback Joe Montana leading the troops, San Francisco won four Super Bowls in the '80s and added a fifth following the 1994 season. They last appeared in the NFL's title game at the end of the 2012 season. The 49ers have been rebuilding in recent years and are building toward their old championship magic after moving to a new stadium in 2014.

WON/LOSS RECORD:
540-464-16 (.546 W-L%)

HOME FIELD:
Levi's Stadium

SUPERFACT

The 49ers are named after the miners who traveled to northern California during the gold rush of the late 1840s. Their first logo was a gold miner wearing a mustache.

Then & Now

TERRELL OWENS 1996–2003 / CARLOS HYDE 2014–present

SUPERFACT

49ers offensive tackle **Joe Staley** has anchored San Francisco's line since he was drafted in 2007. The 315-pound Staley started every game during his rookie season, has played both right and left tackle, is a five-time Pro Bowler and helped the 49ers reach the Super Bowl in 2012. During the season Staley hosts the "Joe Show," a series on the team's website.

TROPHY CASE

Super Bowl titles:
XVI, XIX, XXIII, XXIV, XXIX

Franchise Leaders:

Single-season receptions:
Jerry Rice, 122

Single-season rushing yardage:
Frank Gore, 1,685 yards

Career touchdown receptions:
Jerry Rice, 176

Super Bowl MVPs:
Joe Montana, 3

Seattle
SEAHAWKS

Most football teams have 11 players on the field at all times. When Seattle plays at their home stadium, the Seahawks have what they call "the 12th man" — their legion of very loud fans. The 12th man helped the Seahawks reach back-to-back Super Bowls and make playing in Seattle a miserable and loud experience for opposing teams. Since Pete Carroll became coach in 2010 and then drafted quarterback Russell Wilson two years later, the Seahawks have been one of the steadiest teams in football.

WON/LOSS RECORD:
325-318-1 (.505 W-L%)

HOME FIELD:
CenturyLink Field

SUPERFACT

Seattle's mascot, Blitz, made its debut in 1988. The team later added a sidekick mascot named Boom. Blitz appears at community events, and has been known to skydive.

Then & Now

CULLEN BRYANT 1983–84 / RICHARD SHERMAN 2011–present

SUPERFACT

The Seahawks thought **Russell Wilson** was good. They probably didn't think the 5-foot-11 quarterback would be this good. In his first five years, Wilson led the 'Hawks to two Super Bowls and made three Pro Bowls. Before he was picked by Seattle, the Colorado Rockies of Major League Baseball also drafted Wilson, who played baseball in college. During the 2014 and 2015 offseason, Wilson participated in the Texas Rangers' spring training.

TROPHY CASE

Super Bowl titles: XLVIII

Franchise Leaders:

Single-season rushing touchdowns:
Shaun Alexander, 27

Single-season touchdown passes:
Russell Wilson, 34

Career receiving touchdowns:
Steve Largent, 100

Career rushing touchdowns:
Shaun Alexander, 100

Super Bowl XLVIII MVP:
Malcolm Smith

Tampa Bay
BUCCANEERS

The Buccaneers made their NFL debut in 1976. The Bucs reached the playoffs only three times in their first 20 years. Coach Tony Dungy changed the team's culture in the 1990s and built a championship defense. Head coach Jon Gruden let the defense bring Tampa Bay its first Super Bowl title in after the 2002 season. The Bucs, once again, are contenders in the NFC after drafting star quarterback Jameis Winston in 2015.

WON/LOSS RECORD:
250-393-1 (.389 W-L%)

HOME FIELD:
Raymond James Stadium

SUPERFACT

The team built a replica pirate ship behind one of the end zones at the team's home field. The pirate ship is 103 feet long and fires replica cannons after every Buccaneers score.

Then & Now
VINNY TESTAVERDE 1987–92 / JAMEIS WINSTON 2015–present

SUPERFACT

Wide receiver **Mike Evans** caught more than 1,000 receiving yards in each of his first three years in the NFL. He has become Jameis Winston's preferred target and earned a trip to the Pro Bowl in 2016. He also sponsors "Evans' End Zone Club," where he donates tickets and game day experiences to local charities.

TROPHY CASE

Super Bowl titles: **XXXVII**

Franchise Leaders:

Career passing yardage:
Vinnie Testaverde, 14,820 yards

Single-season receptions:
Keyshawn Johnson, 106

Career points:
Martin Gramatica, 592

Career Pro Bowl selections:
Derrick Brooks, 11

1999 Defensive Player of the Year:
Warren Sapp

Tennessee
TITANS

The Titans were originally the Houston Oilers, but the franchise moved to Tennessee in 1997 and changed its name in 1999. The Titans went to the Super Bowl that same year and fell short, losing in the final seconds at the one yard-line. The Titans haven't made the playoffs since 2008, but the team found their quarterback of the future in Marcus Mariota. The pieces are coming together for another Super Bowl run.

WON/LOSS RECORD:
413-449-6 (.479 W-L%)

HOME FIELD:
Nissan Stadium

SUPERFACT

The Titans are the only pro sports franchise with a (fake) raccoon as its mascot. Fittingly, the raccoon is the state animal of Tennessee. According to his biography on the team's website, T-Rac's favorite food is "anything free."

Then & Now
WARREN MOON 1984–93 / MARCUS MARIOTA 2015–present

TROPHY CASE

Super Bowl Runners-Up: XXXIV

Franchise Leaders:

Single-season rushing yardage:
Chris Johnson, 2,006 yards

Career passing yardage:
Warren Moon, 33,685 yards

Career points:
Al Del Greco, 1,060

Career rushing yardage:
Eddie George, 10,009 yards

Career coaching wins:
Jeff Fisher, 142

SUPERFACT

After a disappointing first season in Philadelphia, running back **DeMarco Murray** was traded to the Titans before the 2016 season. Murray was back to his old self during his first season in Tennessee, exceeding 1,000 yards and providing a safety blanket for quarterback Marcus Mariota. He also earned his third trip to the Pro Bowl.

Washington REDSKINS

The Redskins are one of the league's most valuable and historic teams. They won three Super Bowls in a 10-year span during the 1980s and 1990s, against teams that were stacked with future Hall of Famers. Over Washington's history they have made 24 playoff appearances, and they surprised many experts when they won the NFC East Division in 2015.

WON/LOSS RECORD:
586-572-28 (.506 W-L%)

HOME FIELD:
FedExField

SUPERFACT

The Redskins have the longest-running marching band in the NFL. They've been an all-volunteer band since 1937. They play before games and during halftime, leading the home crowd in renditions of the team's fight song, "Hail to the Redskins."

Then & Now
JOHN RIGGINS 1976–85 / ROBERT KELLEY 2016–present

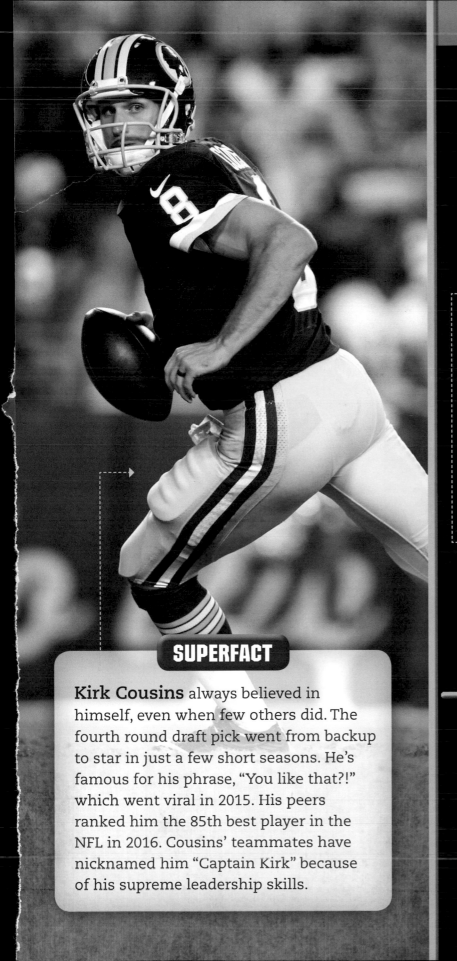

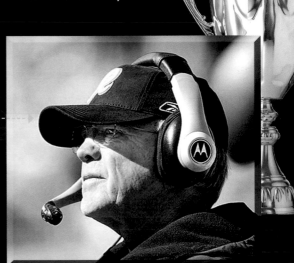

Super Bowl titles:
XVII, XXII, XXVI

Franchise Leaders:

Career passing yardage:
Joe Theismann, 25,206 yards

Career touchdown passes:
Sammy Baugh, 187

Most coaching wins:
Joe Gibbs, 154

Single-season passing yardage:
Kirk Cousins, 4,917 yards

Career rushing touchdowns:
John Riggins, 79

Career interceptions:
Darrell Green, 54

SUPERFACT

Kirk Cousins always believed in himself, even when few others did. The fourth round draft pick went from backup to star in just a few short seasons. He's famous for his phrase, "You like that?!" which went viral in 2015. His peers ranked him the 85th best player in the NFL in 2016. Cousins' teammates have nicknamed him "Captain Kirk" because of his supreme leadership skills.

NFL ALL-TIME LEADERS

RUSHING YARDS

1. Emmitt Smith, 18,355 yards
2. Walter Payton, 16,726 yards
3. Barry Sanders, 15,269 yards
4. Curtis Martin, 14,101 yards
5. LaDainian Tomlinson, 13,684 yards

TOUCHDOWNS SCORED

1. Jerry Rice, 208
2. Emmitt Smith, 175
3. LaDainian Tomlinson, 162
4. Randy Moss, 157
5. Terrell Owens, 156

PASSING TOUCHDOWNS

1. Peyton Manning, 539
2. Brett Favre, 508
3. Drew Brees, 465
4. Tom Brady, 456
5. Dan Marino, 420

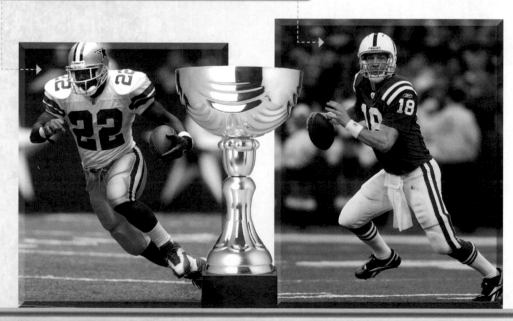

READ MORE

Braun, Eric. *Football's Greatest Quarterbacks*. North Mankato, Minn.: Capstone Press, 2015.

Editors of Sports Illustrated for Kids. *Big Book of Who Football*. Sports Illustrated Kids Big Books Series. New York: Time Home Entertainment, 2015.

Storden, Thom. *Amazing Football Records*. North Mankato, Minn.: Capstone Press, 2015.

INTERNET SITES

Use FactHound to find Internet sites related to this book.

Visit www.facthound.com

Just type in 9781515788522 and go.

INDEX